Proj(

Little Guide To Help Declutter Your Closet

Copyright © 2023

All rights reserved.

DEDICATION

The author and publisher have provided this e-book to you for your personal use only. You may not make this e-book publicly available in any way. Copyright infringement is against the law. If you believe the copy of this e-book you are reading infringes on the author's copyright, please notify the publisher at: https://us.macmillan.com/piracy

Contents

I. What's Project 333?

A closet full of clothes and nothing to wear? If this statement sounds at all familiar to you, it's time for Project 333. Your closet won't be full of clothes anymore, but you WILL have something to wear. And that's not the only benefit of it...

What is Project 333?

Project 333 is a fashion challenge for everyone interested in minimalism. You are invited to pick 33 items from your wardrobe and dress yourself with those items for 3 months.

The idea of this so-called "capsule wardrobe" is not new. In the 1970, the term capsule wardrobe was coined by London based boutique owner Susie Faux. The concept is about dressing with a small collection of seasonally appropriate clothes, shoes and accessories, that can be mixed and matched easily.

The lovely Courtney Carver of Be More With Less turned the idea of dressing with less into Project 333 in 2010 and has inspired thousands of people since then to minimalize their wardrobe – and other parts of their life as well.

As a part of my resolution to make my wardrobe more sustainable, I decided to take on the Project 333 challenge and created my very first capsule wardrobe.

What are benefits of a capsule wardrobe?

There are multiple reasons why a capsule wardrobe is an awesome idea. I listed the most important benefits I have experienced so far while taking this minimalist fashion challenge.

1 – Lower impact on the planet

The (fast) fashion industry is the second most polluting industry on the planet. Creating a capsule wardrobe is one of the ways to lower your carbon footprint and to make your wardrobe more sustainable.

2 – Clutterfree happiness

With so little items, your wardrobe becomes much more organized. You have a clear overview of the options you have. I put all the clothes that aren't included in my capsule wardrobe in a suitcase and then stored the suitcase out of sight. Clutterfree closet = clutterfree mind, I promise you!

3 – Creativity

I am not a fashionista at all (never have been, never will be probably) and I admire the men and women who are. However, Project 333 did spark my creativity. I started combining items I never thought of before.

4 – Favorites only

When you are only 'allowed' to pick 33 items for 3 months, it really makes you think about which clothes you love and want to wear. For me, this is one of the beautiful aspects of a minimalist lifestyle. You get rid of everything that doesn't make you happy and are left only with the things that do.

5 – Happy wallet

A research among East Asian and European consumers conducted by Greenpeace last year showed that up to 50% of the people buy more clothes than they actually need and use. Creating a capsule wardrobe will save you money that you would otherwise spend unnecessarily. The resarch also showed that the excessive shopping does NOT lead to happiness by the way.

How to take this minimalist fashion challenge?

My first Project 333 was supposed to last from May 15th til August 15th. It ended up lasting until the 1st of October!

In the picture you can see all the items (minus my winter coat) that I included in my tiny wardrobe.

Note that accessories and shoes are also included. Items such as socks and underwear however aren't.

Honestly, that was kind of a relief to me. I am all up for minimalism, but including 7 pairs of socks and 7 undies into those 33 items seems like a bridge too far.

5 tips that will turn your Project 333 into a success

If you are excited about creating your own capsule wardrobe, the following tips from my experience might help you.

1 – Take your time to organize your wardrobe

If you have half an hour left before you need to go to your job, that might not be the best moment to organize your Project 333. It took me an entire afternoon to pick the items I wanted to include.

2 – Include enough basics

I have a pair of flower power pants, which I bought about 10 years ago. I still absolutely adore them, but they aren't really easy to combine. Make sure that your capsule wardrobe includes enough basics.

3 – Prepare your capsule wardrobe for events

Think about (possible) events that you might attend in the next 3 months.

I know for example that I have a wedding coming up in August, so my minimalist wardrobe includes one (and only one!) party dress.

4 – Weather proof it

No challenge is the same. One of the biggest influences is the season you are preparing for. As weather in The Netherlands is super unpredictable I carefully chose items that allow me to dress for different weather types. Layers are my new best friends!

After only 10 days of the Project 333 challenge I already had used both a summer dress AND a winter coat.

I guess the 'seasonally appropriate' Susie Faux talked about doesn't really apply to Dutch tiny wardrobes.

5 – Don't be too hard on yourself

If reducing your wardrobe to only 33 items for 3 months is too radical for you, create one that works for you.

Make it 40 items.

Or start with 33 items for one month and see how far you can extend from there. If you are being too hard on yourself, you might give up before you even started. This is not a challenge to suffer!

An almost empty closet and a lot to wear

Having the experience of more than one Project 333 challenge I can honestly say it's one of the best ways to declutter your wardrobe and to stop buying clothes you don't really need.

Go ahead, try it yourself and let me know how it turned out for you!

II. The Rules Of Project 333

What Are The Rules Of Project 333?

 WHAT ARE THE RULES OF PROJECT 333

The rules of Project 333 are fairly simple to follow and apply to your own wardrobe, which is especially encouraging for those who are new to minimalism and are looking for an easy, effective system.

To put it plainly, you probably only wear about 20% of your wardrobe 80% of the time. Cutting out those extra clothes isn't actually a huge loss — you aren't wearing them anyway!

Before trying Project 333, my closet felt like one of those restaurant menus that is the length of a short novel — there were way too many choices! This method simplified my closet in a snap and reduced my decision fatigue when getting ready each day.

In a nutshell, you allow 33 garments into your closet for a period of three months' time. At the end of those first three months, you'll select another set of 33 garments for the next three-month cycle, until you've completed four cycles that take you through the year, and each season.

The idea is that you'll end up with four capsule wardrobes by the completion of the project; one for each season as you create your rotating annual wardrobe. For some people, this means having four totally separate 33-item seasonal capsules, while others allow items to overlap. I prefer to keep it to 33 total items, with many items that work through all seasons.

As an avid minimalist, I only like to keep items in my closet that I know I actively need each season. When I'm sweating up a storm in the North Carolina summer heat, I don't want to have to dig through my snow gear. Project 333 helps you create a rotating capsule that works with the seasonal changes wherever you live!

There are a couple rules that go into making Project 333 that give it its magic. These guidelines are super simple to apply to your own capsule closet.

Rule One: When To Start Project 333

RULE ONE: WHEN TO START PROJECT 333

First things first, it's important to know when to start Project 333. The start time is flexible, which is another thing I personally really love about Courtney's method.

This is a practice that you can start at any time of year. You don't have to wait until you feel "prepared enough" to try out Project 333. It's a system that's great for beginners because it's easy to jump right in on your own timeframe.

Rule Two: Project 333 Duration

RULE TWO: PROJECT 333 DURATION

One of the main rules of project 333 is its duration. The initial process lasts three months, but the overall impact of the process can last an entire lifetime. When you first decide which clothing to keep in your wardrobe, you'll use those clothes for exactly three months. Then, ideally, you'll rinse, repeat, and take on the challenge again in the following three months.

This process can go on for as long as you like! This is another aspect that I really enjoy about Project 333 because it gives me the freedom to try it out for three months, then re-evaluate. I have the capacity to challenge myself for three months, then take a break for the next three months if I need it.

Rule Three: Number Of Clothing Items

RULE THREE: NUMBER OF CLOTHING ITEMS

Another one of the most important rules of Project 333 is the number of clothing items you can keep in your closet. The rules strictly limit you to 33 items of clothing, which sounds like a really limited number at first.

However, I can say that when I tried out Project 333 for the first time, I was pleasantly surprised by how many outfit combos I was actually able to create with only 33 items of clothing! Like I said before, you don't wear as many clothes in your closet as you think. You'll be surprised by how far 33 items can take you.

Rule Four: Which Clothes To Include In The Process

RULE FOUR: WHICH CLOTHES TO INCLUDE IN THE PROCESS

Another interesting aspect of Project 333 is that there are a few exceptions to the clothes you count in your quota. Even though 33 items may seem like a sparse number, not every type of clothing is part of the system. The project tries to include only staple pieces into that 33 number.

PROJECT 333 INCLUDES

Shirts

Pants

Sweaters

Outer Garments

Shoes

Accessories

Jewelry

Rule Five: What Clothes To Exclude

RULE FIVE: WHAT CLOTHES TO EXCLUDE

Project 333 excludes certain clothing items as well. When I was trying out Project 333 for the first time, I was thankful that I didn't have to track my daily wear like my favorite loungewear or pairs of warm socks.

PROJECT 333 EXCLUDES

Underwear

Socks

Sleepwear

Workout Clothes

Loungewear

Steps To Implement Project 333 In Your Daily Life

STEPS TO IMPLEMENT PROJECT 333

It only takes a few simple steps to get started and apply the rules of Project 333 to your own closet and life. I've broken down the practice into five simple steps to help you find your way to a capsule wardrobe you'll never get bored of!

MAKE A PILE OF YOUR CLOTHES

The very first thing I did after deciding to tackle Project 333 was make a huge pile of all of the clothes in my closet, and I mean ALL of them. I know it may sound counterintuitive to make a giant mess when you're trying to declutter, but I assure you this is the best way to go in when you start.

After laying all my clothes out in a pile on my floor, I decided to sort my garments into three categories: A yes pile, a no pile, and a maybe pile. This is one easy way to start thinking through which 33 items you want to include in your wardrobe.

ASK HOW YOUR WARDROBE IMPACTS YOUR LIFESTYLE

It's important to know that Project 333 will manifest differently for everyone depending on their individual lifestyle. There are some clothes that are absolutely essential to some lifestyles, but those same clothes may not really matter to someone else.

For example, some people may need a plethora of workout clothes due to how frequently they hit the gym, while others may want to keep dressier options in their lineup to match their vibrant social life. I work from home during my day, so I don't need a ton of business outfits. For someone else, business wear may make up 80% of their capsule. The 33 pieces of clothing you choose to hold onto should realistically represent your personal lifestyle and habits.

SELECT 33 ITEMS OF CLOTHING

Once you have considered how your lifestyle and habits affect your clothes, it's time to actually make your garment selections. Go through each individual item in your clothing pile and think through whether or not it belongs in your three-month capsule.

There are a few questions I always make sure to ask myself when I take on this part of the process.

WHEN CREATING YOUR CAPSULE, ASK YOURSELF

Have I worn this item in the last three months?

Do I have plans to wear this item in the next 3 months?

Is this a staple piece in my wardrobe?

Is this a special occasion piece in my wardrobe?

Does this garment have a specific use? (bathrobe, snow pants, bathing suit)

Is this a piece I would quickly notice being gone?

Is this item in my typical style and color scheme?

DECIDE WHAT TO DO WITH THE EXTRA CLOTHES

There are lots of options for what to do with the clothes you decide to toss. In any major city, you can easily find access to a donation center that takes hand-me-downs. You can also gift some of the clothes you aren't using to family and friends.

There are tons of minimalist practices out there that can help you decide what to do with all of your extra garments, like Swedish Death Cleaning or the Four-Box Method. I personally really like the four-box method because it splits things up into four straightforward categories that make it easy to quickly sort what you plan to give away.

MARK YOUR TIMELINE ON YOUR CALENDAR

Lastly, it's important that you actually map out when your three-month time period starts and ends so you can visually see your progress. This will help you to stay motivated and encouraged if you start feeling like you want to give up on Project 333.

I use a virtual calendar to keep track of personal goals, but you could also mark your timeline on a paper calendar. As long as you have a visual representation of your goals, you should be set.

Tips For Making Project 333 Work For You

TIPS FOR MAKING PROJECT 333 WORK FOR YOU

When I was trying Project 333 for the first time, I went completely by what Courtney's book said. However, looking back, there are a few simple things that I would do to make the process easier and more enjoyable for me overall.

IF YOU'RE UNSURE, DO A TRIAL RUN

The rules of Project 333 are really manageable, making it a flexible minimalist practice. If you aren't 100% sure that you're ready to start, don't sweat it. I'd suggest doing a trial run week before you actually start your three-month period.

Take up the challenge a week or so early to see how things go. This will help you keep track of the things that did or did not work for you in the first week so you can dive into the challenge for real the following week.

BUILD YOUR WARDROBE AROUND ESSENTIAL PIECES

Like I said before, the key with Project 333 is to build your wardrobe around the pieces that are essential to your specific lifestyle, work culture, and habits. Start with the clothing that you know you will get the most use out of and build your wardrobe up from there.

EMBELLISH WITH DECORATIVE PIECES

After you decipher which pieces of clothing are musts, you're free to embellish your 33-item capsule wardrobe with more decorative pieces. It's important to hit your essential articles of clothing first, and your decorative pieces after.

One mistake that beginners often make with this challenge is immediately choosing some of their favorite, more flashy clothing items just because they love them, and neglecting to leave room for the basic pieces that can be worn multiple ways.

TAKE NOTES ON WHAT WORKS AND WHAT DOESN'T

One of the things I didn't do the first time I took this challenge — which I'll always do from now on — is take notes as I go through the process. I keep a bullet journal with me when I try any new minimalist challenge so that I can track the things that work best and the things that didn't work at all. This helps me adjust my process or better prepare for the challenge in the future.

Should You Try Project 333?

As a guy who is deeply inspired by making things as simple as possible, I am a big fan of Project 333. I've seen it improve my life and mentality in a plethora of ways and would highly recommend taking this challenge on!

III. A Project 333 Recap – the pros and cons of a seasonal wardrobe challenge

Three months flew by a lot faster than I'd anticipated, which only seems to highlight how quickly this year has gone; I mean, when did it become June already and when did I become one of those people who *constantly* talks about how fast time is screaming past us? I mean, way to state the obvious....

As a person who once baulked at the thought of even contemplating a wardrobe challenge, it's fair to say that my perception and ability to live with fewer things has changed dramatically in the last few years. With Project 333 now done and dusted, it seemed like the perfect opportunity to share with you all my thoughts on this wardrobe challenge, and run through some of the pros and cons of living with a capsule or minimal wardrobe. So I'm just going to warn you now, *this is going to be a long one…*

The thing that surprised me most? I didn't cheat – not even once (unless wearing my Hope grand sweater as pyjamas counts…) – although I *did* make the odd change to my capsule wardrobe. As it would so obviously turn out, no matter how much you plan in advance, you can't quite predict how the weather is going to turn a week ahead, or have the faintest clue as to how cold it might possibly be two months out.

Within the first week, I was already making changes to my capsule, which wasn't exactly what I had in mind given I spent a good two months slowly refining and editing down my choices… While my capsule largely stayed the same, I started to think a bit more about which pieces were the most dynamic, and that I could still wear two months on when the weather was likely to be cooling down.

It started off with the Karen Walker grey cardigan, which felt too similar to the Ashley Fogel one I'd already started wearing on a daily basis, and the white Ashley Fogel jumper as I wanted a little additional variety. Then I decided that the trench coat wasn't necessary (a fail on more than one count..), nor was the apricot-hued blazer, or the blush skirt. I opted for a pair of black denim in lieu of the indigo pair I'd initially chosen, and realised a month in that one of my skirts had been at the dry cleaners for at least four weeks and was unlikely to be joining the rest of my capsule pieces anytime soon.

I ended up making the following additions to my capsule; a printed skirt from Josh Goot which works just as well with tights as it does with bare legs. A grey wool flannel pencil skirt from Karen Walker which I could get away with both in the office with a silk blouse or on the weekend with a loose jumper. A black woollen skirt from T by Alexander Wang due to its simplicity and how easy it is to throw on. A pair of black skinny stretch denim jeans from J Brand which feel almost like wearing a pair of tights when they're on. And lastly, a navy raw wool coat from COS as the temperature dropped considerably in early May, and this turned out to be a piece I wore to and from the office every. single. day.

Somehow, I ended up with a total of 32 capsule items to wear over the three month period (or 30, when you take into account that two of the pieces were worn a total of once each…); which given my hesitation to stop at just 33 was a huge triumph for me, especially as on any given day I have between 80-100 pieces in my wardrobe to choose from. I definitely found this challenge to be a lot less difficult than I expected, and I suspect it was down to a few key things in addition to a couple of lessons I learnt along the way…

1. Start to form your capsule around core wardrobe basics;

Think of this as your staple-go-with-everything pieces – the ones which you can throw on with just about anything. For me, this meant starting with things like a classic leather jacket, a great pair of denim, a sleeveless blouse, a black blazer and a loose fitting cami.

2. Choose pieces that you feel good in and enjoying wearing;

There isn't much point spending three months of your life with a capsule wardrobe that you don't **love**, so focus on including pieces which fit well, are good quality, and that you enjoy and feed good wearing.

3. Develop a uniform… of sorts;

Having a few different uniforms or 'proportions' to base your daily outfits around not only helps with selecting the pieces for a capsule wardrobe but also provides a good foundation for day to day wear.

4. Be prepared for a turn in the weather;

One thing I learnt over the last three months was how impossible it is to know for sure how warm or cold it will be over any given season. Make sure to keep a space or two free for those occasions or focus on building in layers.

5. Stick to a colour palette;

I've said it before and I'll say it again, but sticking to a colour palette (whether it be neutrals like I tend to go for, or bright and colourful prints if that's your jam) makes the whole challenge so much more painless.

6. Avoid the shops and don't be tempted by sales;

This has always been my downfall in the past, as I'd usually continue shopping at my usual speed when attempting to get through 30×30 or wear a more 'limited' selection of my wardrobe. This season, I added so few things to my wardrobe that I wasn't tempted to throw on something new and shiny, and managed to stick to the items within my capsule wardrobe.

In terms of the pros and cons of Project 333, it is without a shadow of a doubt much easier to get dressed in the morning. Opening the closet (or rifling through the clothing rack in my study) was a lot less stressful as I had a defined set of items which I knew worked together quite seamlessly. There wasn't a single day that I felt like I had nothing to wear, even when I was wearing the same or similar combinations regularly. In a way, it was oddly freeing. While I definitely didn't 'dress up' as much as I could have (flats were my shoe of choice), I always felt put together; I was always happy with what I was wearing, and I got to wear my favourite pieces all the time. The changes to a look were a lot more subtle but you could easily mix in a bold necklace, a printed scarf, or a quirky pair of shoes.

On the flipside, you'll be wearing *the same* pieces day in and day out, without a lot of variety.

Your uniform will become your look, and your clothing – regardless of quality – will undergo a lot more wear and tear over a three month period than usual. As an example, I noticed that my Everlane cashmere sweater developed a bit of pilling (easily fixed, or course!), and I got a small hole in my Karen Walker silk stripe blouse.

If having a full wardrobe at your disposal is something you would struggle to give up, if not only for the variety but also for the freedom of being able to wear any given style or look any day of the week, then it probably goes without saying that this challenge will be a huge struggle for you.

IV. How To Create A Capsule Wardrobe

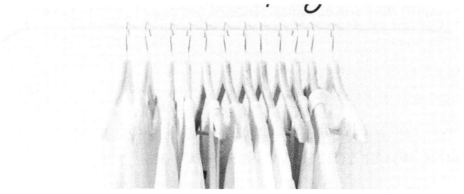

FAST FASHION'S ENVIRONMENTAL IMPACT

First, let's talk about fashion's impact on the environment.

It's estimated that one garbage truck of clothes is burned or landfilled every second. Fashion is water-intensive, taking about 2,000 gallons of water to make a single pair of jeans, and is also a huge water polluter—textile dyeing is the world's 2nd largest source of water pollution.

Those are just the issues with producing clothes. Oftentimes when we're finished with our clothes, we feel like we're doing the right thing by donating them. But oftentimes, those clothes are shipped to Africa where they destroy the local textile businesses or still end up in the landfill.

THE GOAL

To combat the environmental effects of fast fashion, the best things we can do are:

Use what you already have

Shop secondhand

Choose clothes made from natural fibers that are made to last

USING WHAT YOU HAVE – PROJECT 333

To breathe some new life into your wardrobe, consider taking the Project 333 Challenge! Project 333 is a challenge to use 33 articles of clothing and accessories for 3 months. So, basically a season. For example, you would choose clothes for the months of October, November, and December.

This includes:

Clothes

Jewelry

Belts

Hats

Scarves

Purses

Shoes

This does not include:

Undergarments

Workout clothes (unless you wear them as your daily clothes)

Pajamas

To get started, think about your general style. For me, this is floral dresses or all black with a pop of cheetah print. For my husband, it's muted Earth tones. If you don't know your specific style yet, then start with a color palette. Choose a base color like black, brown or navy. You'll already have a lot of these colors in your closet because most people fall into one of these three base colors.

Then build from there.

Which colors are you most drawn to?

Being an ocean lover, I'm drawn to blues and greens.

Then think about the styles or cuts you like.

I'm a skinny jean, structured and fitted dress type of person.

If you can't pin point the styles you like, then think about your favorite articles of clothing that you wear every week.

Next, start putting together outfits.

For years, each season, I put together 5 outfits that I wear each week to work in the same order. I thought people would notice but NO

ONE noticed. I would get an occasional compliment on what I was wearing but no one knew until I mentioned I wear the same 5 outfits in a row.

As you're putting together outfits, if you find that you have 35 or even 40 articles of clothing, no worries. Use 33 as a guide. If 40 works for you, cool.

After you've selected your items, put all the other clothes away, or move them to the back of your clothes or turn the hangers around. Whatever you do, you want to make them "off limits" to you for the rest of the challenge.

MY FALL CAPSULE WARDROBE

Since I've been minimizing and pruning my wardrobe for so long, I've included workout clothes and pajamas in my 33 articles of clothing, shoes, and accessories. In the Bay Area, the fall can be both really hot and cold. Especially in the inland areas, it can be near freezing in the mornings and swing into the 80s and 90s in the afternoons. So, since I'll be using this capsule for the months of October, November, and December, I have some warm weather items and some cold weather items.

Here are the items in my capsule wardrobe starting at the top left corner:

Cotton Camisole Top

Cotton Tank Top For Running

Silk Shirt For Work

Cotton Hoodie

Wool Coat

Leggings For Running

Work Pants

Cotton Long Sleeve Shirt For Running

Silk Sweater For Work

Cotton Sweater

Puffer Jacket

Cheetah Belt

Cotton Shorts

Jeans

Sweater For Work

Sweater

Jacket For Work

Wave Ring

Project 333

Emerald Ring

Gold Bracelet

Long Necklace For Work

Work Tote

Everyday Purse

Running Shoes

Casual Silk Dress

Silk Work Dress

Sweater Dress

Pj Dress

Cotton Work Dress

Cheetah Wedges

Flip Flops

Flats

Work Heels

Here are a few outfits I put together with these pieces. This is one of my weekly work outfits. I get a lot of compliments on this dress! I pair it with some black heels and a black cotton jacket since it's freezing in my office. I have a black tote bag to carry my laptop back and forth from my house. And lastly, I have a gold bracelet that I'm always wearing.

Here's another work outfit. Black pants with a black silk shirt which has a flower on the shoulder. I add the pops of cheetah print through the belt and wedges. And add a gold necklace to match the gold bracelet I always have on.

Here's a casual outfit I would wear on a Friday to work or if it's a
little cooler while running errands.

And here's a casual outfit if it's a little warmer outside.

And finally, here's something I would wear on a date night with my husband.

BENEFITS OF PROJECT 333

The point of the Project 333 challenge is to show you that you have plenty to wear and that you can dress yourself with a fraction of your closet. By defining what you need, it will prevent you from continually adding to your wardrobe. Basically, the challenge shows you what "enough" looks like. If you finally have enough clothes, you'll stop shopping. And if you stop shopping to add to your wardrobe, you'll stop feeding the cycle of fast fashion.

SHOP SECONDHAND

After you've figured out your 33-ish pieces, you might need an item or two to complete your capsule. No problem. Try to find that item secondhand. You can try your local thrift or consignment shop, if you want to try things on before purchasing them.

Or you can try finding your favorite brands on online consignment shops like

Project 333

ThredUp:

TheRealReal

Poshmark

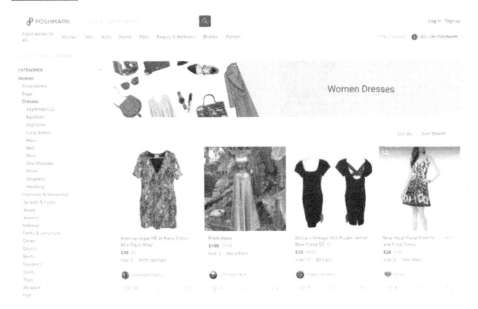

Nearly, all of my work clothes are from theRealReal. Like I mentioned previously, I like floral dresses, this silk DVF dress was perfect for me:

Sorry this item sold out! Shop similar items while they're still available.

DIANE VON FURSTENBERG
Silk Mini Dress
Size: M I US 6
$50.00
20% Off Use Code REAL
Est. Retail $460.00

SOLD

Add to Wait List

Description

- Diane von Furstenberg Silk Sheath Dress
- Purple
- Printed
- Short Sleeve with Bateau Neckline

Designer Fit: Dresses by Diane von Furstenberg typically fit true to size.

Details

By shopping secondhand you can help reduce the demand for new clothes and save money! This DVF dress was a perfect example. Brand new, these dresses are $500+ and I bought it for less than $50. (There's usually a 20% off code at the top of the screen with theRealReal. It applies on most but not all items.)

CHOOSE NATURAL FIBER CLOTHES MADE TO LAST

If you can't find what you need secondhand, then choose clothes that are made to last from natural fibers like cotton, hemp, silk, and linen. As I've mentioned before, when we wash our clothes, it's estimated that we wash 700,000 microfibers for every load of laundry. These microfibers are too small for wastewater treatment plants to catch so they flow into our ocean.

If the fibers are made from natural materials, then they will degrade in the ocean. If they are made from synthetic materials like polyester, nylon, or acrylic, then that load of laundry is sending more plastics into our ocean.

A lot of my basics, like tank tops, socks, and workout shorts are from Pact, an organic cotton clothing brand.

The only thing with Pact is that if you like something, scoop it up! They're continually changing their product line so when they run out of an item, they might not make it again. There have been several times I bought one of something I LOVED, only to find out they stopped making it when I went to purchase a second one.

I have two of these sweaters (one for work and a larger size to be cozy at home) and…you guessed it…they don't make it anymore.

RINSE & REPEAT IN JANUARY

At the beginning of 2022 when you've finished your first Project 333 Challenge, hopefully, you'll realize you don't need a lot of clothes to dress yourself. As you repeat the challenge, you'll refine your style and capsule wardrobes down to the clothes that you love and fit you well. Along the way you'll start letting go of the trendy items, or clothes that just didn't fit your body or style.

Before donating those clothes, consider adding them to your emergency bag. If it still fits, it will probably work for an emergency. I talk more about emergency bag contents in this post:

If your emergency bag is set, then consider selling the items on one of the three consignment sites mentioned above. I did this while I was curating my closet down to it's perfect size.

Now, the goal wasn't to make money. It was really to ensure that it would actually be used again. Like I mentioned above, donated clothes still oftentimes end up in the landfill or shipped to Africa. Another option would be to do a clothing swap with some friends. The more we can prolong the use of our clothes the better!

RECAP

Long story short, the best thing we can do to fight the environmental effects of fast fashion is to limit our consumption of new clothes. The more we can use what we have, shop secondhand, and choose clothes that will last us longer, the less waste we create.

V. Project 333 For Kids

Every parent knows there are mountains of laundry involved with kids. The secret to getting through this is <u>creating a capsule wardrobe</u> inspired by Courtney Carver's <u>Project 333</u>.

The goal is to minimize kids clothing in your house in order to make laundry day and getting dressed much more simple.

Why have a capsule wardrobe?

In a capsule wardrobe, <u>each piece is carefully and intentionally chosen</u>. Ideally your entire wardrobe would consist of articles of clothing that are comfortable, fit well, and can be mixed and matched.

This takes the stress out of dressing in the morning and ensures you're never standing in a crowded closet feeling like there is "nothing to wear". These 33 items can take you from home, to school, to a party, and anywhere you need to be during the 3 months. Sounds great, doesn't it?

Project 333 for Kids

Here is an example based on what I've used for my daughters in the past. For Project 333, socks, underwear, and pajamas aren't included in the list.

5 T-shirts

3 long sleeved shirts

6 bottoms (shorts, pants)

2 light cardigans

3 heavier sweaters

2 dresses (or extra playclothes)

2 fancy dresses (or nice outfits for special occasions)

4 pairs of shoes (sneakers, sandals, dressy shoes, rubber boots)

1 hat

1 pair of sunglasses

1 jacket

1 pair of splash pants

1 bathing suit

1 backpack

Does Project 333 really work for kids?

It can be difficult trying to stay on top of both the daily outfit changes and constantly changing sizes as kids grow. Therefore the criteria for kids capsule wardrobes might look different than it does for adults.

For example, you might be less worried about style and investment pieces and more about what fits them and can be cleaned easily. Here are some criteria for choosing which pieces to use for your child's Project 333 wardrobe.

1. Make a laundry schedule.

If you're worried that 33 items won't be enough, make a laundry schedule. This might seem like an odd step to begin with, but think about how often you do laundry and then work around this. For example, if you do laundry once a week then you'll obviously need at least a week's worth of clothing. 33 items will cover that many outfits, even with extra outfit changes during the day.

If you find yourself doing laundry twice a week, you might get away with having less—or you'll have even more options. If you don't have set times to do laundry, think about implementing this so it becomes more organized. You'll discover that Project 333 can fit a lifestyle with children.

2. Keep tops and bottoms that mix and match.

If you have too much and are trying to pare down, I suggest keeping items that easily mix and match with each other. I do this by choosing pants that go with most of the tops: jeans, khakis, or colors that match a lot of existing items.

That one mint-green-butterfly-patterned outfit that has pieces which specifically need to be together? Yeah, that's the one to go. When everything goes together it makes it simple to grab a top and a bottom. And if you have kids who insist on dressing themselves, then you'll have the added bonus that they'll actually pick things that match.

3. Store off-season items.

Eliminate the chaos of having everything in the closet or dresser at once. Only keep the items for this season, and then store and label any off-season clothes. I use a big Rubbermaid bin which sits on the top shelf in their closet. This also applies to any clothes that they will grow into soon.

However, don't get carried away with storing for seasons, otherwise this will become another source of clutter. Depending on the climate you live in, perhaps organizing twice per year could be enough: a Spring/Summer season and Fall/Winter season.

4. Pass on clothing.

Other people might approach this differently, but I choose to give away clothes as soon as my children grow out of them. One way that clutter accumulates quickly in homes is when we keep items "just in case".

I've been lucky enough to have a lot of people give me second-hand clothes for the kids, and I buy clothes only when there's a gap in their wardrobe and a specific item is needed. Since I've been given so much, I'd like to pass on things to other people too.

I'd rather give items to someone who definitely needs it now, than keep things for my own 'someday, maybe'. (The easiest time to go through clothes is when the seasons change since you'll have to adjust their wardrobe anyway.)

5. Keep closets simple.

<u>I keep the kids' clothing in bins</u> instead of a dresser. Each child has one box for tops (T-shirts, cardigans, and sweaters), one box for bottoms (shorts, pants, and dresses), one box for underwear (including socks and bathing suit), and one for pajamas.

Instead of hanging or folding clothes, I simply sort the clean clothes into the correct box. This makes it easy to put clean clothes away, and easy to find things in the morning. When I move the boxes onto the floor, the kids can sort their own clean laundry.

Make some space in your closets, house, and family life. Apply Project 333 to your child's clothing and see how simplicity can make your family's life more calm, stress-free, and organized with less stuff and more life.

VI. Project 333 For First Time

Lots of us are used to having at least 40 or 50 garments available for the current season, so the idea of limiting all of our clothing AND accessories to 33 pieces seems daunting! But 1 thing that I'm pretty sure the creator of Project 333 would agree with – you should just start *somewhere*, and move on as you feel comfortable! Therefore, I decided to build a wardrobe template that includes 30 garments – still fewer than many of us are used to seeing in our closets, but a pretty comfortable number...

Project 333

Cluster 1	Cluster 2	Cluster 3	Cluster 4	Cluster 5	Cluster 6
2nd layer	2nd layer	2nd layer	2nd layer	2nd layer	2nd layer
top	top	top	top	top	top
top	top	top	top	top	top
top or bottom	top or bottom	top or bottom	top or bottom	top or bottom	top or bottom
bottom	bottom	bottom	bottom	bottom	bottom

When I look at this template, it seems like a huge number of pieces! But once you start pulling items out of your closet, it could fill pretty quickly.

I'm planning this wardrobe more or less on what I might consider for my own Project 333 this autumn, more or less. When I get my choices settled I will share them, but for now this is a kind of sort of approximation of how I would approach things.

THE ESSENTIAL CLUSTER

I think of this first cluster as being the pieces of clothing that I would grab in I literally had to cram a few things into a backpack and live in them for a week or two...

Cluster 1

sweater – Halogen; tee shirt – BP.; cardigan – Halogen; pants –
Eileen Fisher; jeans – Eileen Fisher

There's not any variety here to speak of, and it's strictly
monochromatic, but one could go for quite a long time with just
these 5 pieces, in a pinch... But let's give more options in our
neutral by using our 2nd Cluster as a Supplemental Essentials

grouping (which could also be called the Corduroy Cluster!)...

THE CORDUROY PANTS

Cluster 2

turtleneck – Lands' End; tee shirt – Lands' End; blazer – Eileen Fisher; corduroy pants – Lands' End; corduroy skirt – Lands' End

At this point, you're going to look pretty somber if this is your wardrobe, but this is an excellent background for amazing jewelry or beautiful scarves. If you traveled with these 10 garments, you'd be in great shape!

But for those of us who live in black, there are still some essentials missing! A simple button-front cardigan, which can be worn over another top, or worn on its own, is SO useful... A couple of button-front shirts (which can be worn over a tee shirt, or under a sweater, or BOTH AT THE SAME TIME!) are useful, a pretty black sweater opens up dressier possibilities, and jeans that aren't skin-tight... why not?

THE BUTTON-FRONT CLUSTER

Cluster 3

flannel shirt – Uniqlo; shirt – Uniqlo; cardigan – Uniqlo; sweater – 1901; jeans – Frame

Let's pause for a moment to see where we are in our wardrobe-building process!

Cluster 1	Cluster 2	Cluster 3	Cluster 4	Cluster 5	Cluster 6
			2nd layer	2nd layer	2nd layer
			top	top	top
			top	top	top
			top or bottom	top or bottom	top or bottom
			bottom	bottom	bottom

You might absolutely abhor the idea of this much black in your wardrobe, but this is an undeniably versatile assortment...

Still, for most people, it's way past time to introduce some color! So taking my cue from the plaid flannel shirt above, I'm going to introduce some blue, to brighten things up. This is also a good time to find a white shirt, and maybe another printed or patterned shirt...

THE BLUE SWEATER CLUSTER

Project 333

Cluster 4

tee – Lands' End; white shirt – Lands' End; sweater – Lands'
End; shirt – Banana Republic; skirt – Chaus

65

At this point in the wardrobe-choosing process, our mythical heroine has realized that she really wants to include her grey and black marled cardigan in this wardrobe! So she makes a point to choose 5 garments that aren't black, but which can be worn with her black things.

THE GREY CLUSTER

Cluster 5

tee – Lands' End; grey tee – Eileen Fisher; cardigan – Banana Republic; corduroy pants – L.L.Bean; sweater – Ralph Lauren

She's in a good spot! But she pauses for a bit and thinks about what 3 months is going to include… This wardrobe probably isn't going to be worn until the beginning of October, so that means the Thanksgiving weekend, and all of the winter holidays around the end of the year. Better include some dressy things! (This mythical heroine has a robust social life...)

THE SOCIAL LIFE CLUSTER

Cluster 6

knit dress – Land's End; chiffon dress – Eileen Fisher; lace dress – Uniqlo; sequined tee – P.A.R.O.S.H.; beaded cardigan – CO

Whew! Choosing these pieces takes quite a bit of time, but there's a profound tranquility and focus to having such a carefully edited wardrobe:

VII. Choosing Accessories For Project 333

Before we dive into accessories, let's remember what our final color scheme was (remember, I had to change the colors halfway through building the wardrobe!):

Japanese Irises Scarf

Feminine but not twee, casual but not messy. Classic navy, gold and ivory with accents of leafy green. Simple styles in soft fabrics.

Japanese Irises Scarf – The Metropolitan Museum of Art Store

And the wardrobe was this; yes, I could easily have re-arranged these items to put the camel-colored items into the 2nd row to be the 2nd neutral. Proof that these templates are guidelines and NOT rules!

The 4 by 4 Wardrobe

First Core of 4
2 tops, 2 bottoms.
All the same neutral color

2nd Core of 4
2 tops, 2 bottoms in a 2nd neutral, or more items in your first neutral

Mileage 4
4 tops, in anything that goes with your first 8 garments; introduce prints, patterns or accent colors! You have to wear a top every day...

Expansion 4
At least 2 tops, with maybe a dress or bottoms.
Any area where you feel insecure should be addressed here.

cardigan – Chelsea28; navy tee – Lands' End; ponte knit pants – Uniqlo; jeans – L.L.Bean; striped jacket – The Great; ivory tee – Lands' End; navy flannel shirt – Uniqlo; jacquard pants – Scotch & Soda; silk shirt – J.Crew; plaid shirt – L.L.Bean; camel shirt – Uniqlo; Henley – L.L..Bean; green metallic sweater – Sandro; ivory cardigan – Lands' End; camel sweater – J.Crew; camel pants – Uniqlo

I've been thinking about accessories a lot… Maybe we can organize them the same kind of way we organize clothes? Let's start with the stuff that most of us MUST have (although bear in mind that there is NO SINGLE ITEM in the world that every woman needs. NONE.).

Essential

watch – Skagen; bag – AEVHA London; booties – Sam
Edelman; loafers – Børn

For those of us who can walk, shoes are critical. A bag is
important, but not essential, for most women. And even though
you can tell the time on your phone, you don't want to be one of
those people glued to your phone… (and miss the chance to

wear a pretty watch?)

So I was picturing this as an organizing tool:

16 Accessories

Essential - shoes, a watch and a bag				
Ornament - jewelry				
Softness and Color - scarves or jewelry				
Expression - things that you particularly love				

Next up I was thinking about just 4 pieces of jewelry. Many of us would have a LOT more pieces than this in our core wardrobe, but a surprising number of women wear the same handful of jewelry every day... Maybe this template helps us to at least remember the core pieces we most want for the upcoming season – or it helps us remember to pack jewelry! (I did, once, forget all of mine... I managed quite well with what I wore on the flight!)

Ornament

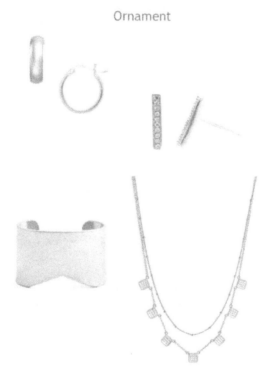

Project 333

hoop earrings – Argento Vivo; diamond bar earrings – Bony Levy; cuff bracelet – Sole Society; necklace – Anna Beck

The template begins to look better, eh?

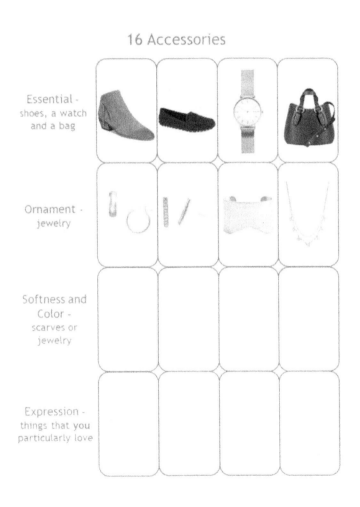

16 Accessories

Essential - shoes, a watch and a bag

Ornament - jewelry

Softness and Color - scarves or jewelry

Expression - things that you particularly love

Of course there will be scarves! But I've also kept the option open that one could add additional jewelry, with colored stones or enamel, if 4 scarves seems like too many…

Softness and Color

tiger eye earrings – Kendra Scott; houndstooth scarf – BP.; floral scarf – Ted Baker London; sapphire earrings – Bloomingdale's

This really is taking shape…

16 Accessories

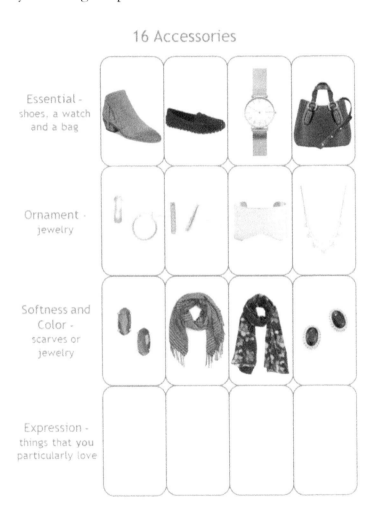

Now, the heroine of every wardrobe gets to choose items that really are important to her. I would probably add another pair of shoes and more scarves, but that's just me; you get to include anything you want!

Expression

crossbody bag – Dorothy Perkins; sneakers – Sudini; scarf –
Stella McCartney; sunglasses – Smith

NOW, this looks good! (if I do say so myself…)

16 Accessories

Let's now revisit the outfits from Monday, but add some

accessories to see how much better things look when they're "finished."

Project 333

83

Made in the USA
Las Vegas, NV
30 April 2025

21522561R00049